THE SACRIFICE

FRANK BIDART

THE SACRIFICE

 RANDOM HOUSE · NEW YORK

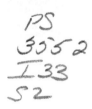
Portions of this work were previously published
in the *New Republic*, *Paris Review* and *Ploughshares*.

The prose passages in "The War of Vaslav Nijinsky" are based on
writings of Romola Nijinsky, Richard Buckle, Serge Lifar, and
Maurice Sandoz. Grateful acknowledgment is made to Simon &
Schuster for permission to reprint excerpts from *Nijinsky* by
Romola Nijinsky, Copyright 1934, © 1961 by Romola Nijinsky.
Reprinted by permission of Simon & Schuster, a Division of
Gulf & Western Corporation. All other rights
controlled by Eric Glass Ltd, London.

Library of Congress Cataloging in Publication Data
Bidart, Frank, 1939–
The sacrifice.
Contents: The war of Vaslav Nijinsky—For Mary Ann
Youngren—Catullus—[etc.]
I. Title.
PS3552.I33S2   1983   811'.54   83-3377
ISBN 0-394-53297-X

CONTENTS

. . . the speculative Good Friday in place of the historic Good Friday. Good Friday must be speculatively re-established in the whole truth and harshness of its Godforsakenness.

—Hegel

THE
SACRIFICE

THE WAR OF
VASLAV NIJINSKY

Still gripped by the illusion of an horizon;
overcome with the finality of a broken tooth;
suspecting that habits are the only salvation,

—the Nineteenth Century's
guilt, *World War One,*

was danced

by Nijinsky on January 19, 1919.

.   .   .

... I am now reading *Ecce Homo.* Nietzsche
is *angry* with me—;

he hates "the Crucified One."

But he did not live through War—;
when the whole world painted its face

with blood.

Someone must expiate the blood.

.   .   .

No. Let what is past
be forgotten. Let even the blood

be forgotten—; there *can be no* "expiation."

Expiation is not necessary.

Suffering has made me what I am,—

I must not regret; or judge; or
struggle to escape it

in the indifference of (the ruthless
ecstasy of)
        CHANGE; "my endless RENEWAL"; BECOMING.

—That is Nietzsche.

He wants to say "Y*es*" to life.

I am not Nietzsche. I am the bride of Christ.

       .   .   .

He was planning a new and original ballet. It was to be a picture
of sex life, with the scene laid in a *maison tolérée.* The chief char-
acter was to be the owner—once a beautiful *cocotte,* now aged and
paralyzed as a result of her debauchery; but, though her body is a
wreck, her spirit is indomitable in the traffic of love. She deals with
all the wares of love, selling girls to boys, youth to age, woman to
woman, man to man.

    When he danced it, he succeeded in transmitting the whole
scale of sex life.

       .   .   .

—Many times Diaghilev wanted me
to make love to him

as if he were
a woman—;

I did. I *refuse* to
regret it.
            At first, I felt humiliated for him,—

he saw this. He got angry
and said, "I enjoy it!"

Then, more calmly, he said,

"Vatza, we must not *regret* what we *feel*."

—I REGRETTED

                what I FELT . . . Not

making love, but that since the beginning
I wanted to *leave* him . . .
                        That I stayed

out of "GRATITUDE,"—
                and FEAR OF LIFE,—
                                and AMBITION . . .

That in my soul,
                I did *not* love him.

Now my wife wants to have
a second child. I am frightened;

the things a human being must learn,—
the things a child

must *learn* he FEELS,—

frighten me! I know people's faults

because in my soul,
                    I HAVE COMMITTED THEM.

The man who chops wood for us
was speaking, this morning, in the kitchen,

to my wife. As I passed in the hallway
I heard

whispering—; and LISTENED . . .

He said that as a child
in his village at Sils Maria

he worked for the writer, *Nietzsche*—;
he felt he must tell her

that just before the "famous man"
was taken away, INSANE,

he acted and looked

AS I DO NOW.

I can choose *"life"* for myself;—

but must I, again, again,
AGAIN,—
                    for *any other* creature?

                .   .   .

The Durcals arrived in St. Moritz, and were invited to tea. Asked what he had been doing lately, Vaslav put on a worldly air, leaned back on the sofa and said,

"Well, I composed two ballets, I prepared a new program for the next Paris season, and lately—I have played a part. You see, I am an artist; I have no troupe now, so I miss the stage. I thought it would be rather an interesting experiment to see how well I could act, and so for six weeks I played the part of a lunatic; and the whole village, my family, and even the physicians apparently believed it. I have a male nurse to watch me, in the disguise of a *masseur*."

Romola was overcome, torn between anger and relief. She was confirmed in her supposition that her fears had been groundless when the male nurse came, after ten days, to assure her from his long experience that her husband was completely sane.

.   .   .

—Let me explain to you
what "*guilt*" is . . .

When I joke with my wife, and say,
"I think I will go back to Russia
and live as a peasant—"

she jokes back, and says,
"Do as you like! I will
divorce you, and marry
                        a manufacturer . . ."

She looks at me, and I look at her.

What is terrible

is that I am serious—; and *she* is serious . . .

She is right, of course,—

                                      I do *not* have the right

to make her live differently, without servants,
rich friends, elegant clothes—
without her good and sane *habits*;

do not have the right even to try
to *re-make* her . . .

But does *she* then have the right
to make *me* live like this, JUDGED, surrounded by
those who cannot understand or *feel* me,—

                                           like a manufacturer? . . .

She is angry, as I am angry.

We both are *right*—; and both angry . . .

Soon, she feels guilty, feels that she
has failed me—;
                         and I too
feel guilty . . .

The GUILT comes from NOWHERE.

Neither of us has done wrong!

But I am a good actor—and reassure her
that I love her; am indeed happy; and that
nothing will change . . .

I *want* to be a *good husband.*

Still, I am guilty.

                 . . . Why am I guilty?

My life is *FALSE*.

.   .   .

I know the psychology of lunatics;
if you don't contradict them, they like you.

But I am not insane.

My brother was insane. He died
in a lunatic asylum.

The reason I *know* I am *NOT* insane
is because, unlike my brother,

I *feel guilt.*

The insane do not feel guilt.

My brother was a dancer. He was older than I,
but still in the *corps* when I became
a soloist. He was ashamed, and jealous;

he went insane.

When the doctors questioned him, he showed
astonishing courage,—
                                    he thought that everyone
in the company was paid

by the secret police, to gather
evidence against our family . . .

He displayed cunning, and stoic
fortitude, under the questions.

Even when he thought he faced death,
he lied
to protect my mother.

When he was taken away,
she cried, and cried . . .
                    She cried
visiting him,—

but that didn't make him feel GUILTY . . .

My wife thought because
I wore a large *cross* on my neck in the village,—

and told her certain dishes
served at our table were poisoned,—

I was insane.

But I *knew* that my actions
frightened her—; and I suffered.

Nietzsche was insane. He knew
we killed God.

                . . . This is the *end* of the story:

though He was dead, God was clever
and strong. God struck back,—

AND KILLED US.

If I *act* insane, people will call me
"mad clown," and forgive
                    even the truth—;

the insane feel anxiety and horror,

but are RELEASED
from GUILT . . .

I only want to know
things I've learned like this,—

these things I cannot *NOT* know.

.   .   .

His other ballet remained unfinished. It was his own life put into
a choreographic poem: a youth seeking truth through life, first as
a pupil, open to all artistic suggestions, to all the beauty that life
and love can offer; then his love for the woman, his mate, who
successfully carries him off.

He set it in the period of the High Renaissance. The youth is a
painter; his Master one of the greatest artists of the period, part
Genius and part Politician, just as Diaghilev seemed to him to be.
This Master advances him, and defends his daring work from the
attacks of colleagues, as long as he is a student; then he falls in
love, and the Master bitterly rejects not only him but his work.

.   .   .

—Last night, once again, I nearly
abandoned my autobiographical ballet . . .

The plot has a good beginning
and middle,—
        THE PUZZLE

is the end . . .

The *nights* I spend—

           reading and improving
Nietzsche, analysing and then abandoning

my life, working on the *Great Questions*

like WAR and GUILT and GOD
and MADNESS,—

I rise from my books, my endless, fascinating
researches, notations, projects,

dazzled.
        —Is this happiness? . . .

I have invented a far more
accurate and specific notation for dance;

it has taken me two months
to write down the movement in my ten-minute

ballet, *L'Après-midi d'un Faune* . . .

There is a MORAL here

about how LONG you must live with
the consequences of a SHORT action,—

but I don't now feel
MORAL.
        Soon I shall begin

Le Sacre du Printemps—; which
is longer . . .

I can understand the pleasures of War.

In War—
        where *killing* is a virtue: *camouflage*
a virtue: *revenge* a virtue:
pity a weakness—
        the world rediscovers

a *guiltless* PRE-HISTORY

"civilization" condemns . . .

In 1914, I was assured
the War would end in six weeks;

the Germans, in the summer, thought
they would enter Paris by the fall.

But the War
                     was NOT an accident.

CUSTOM, and his Children,—

Glory. Honor. Privilege. Poverty.
Optimism. "The Balance of Power,"—

for four years

dug a large, long hole
(—a TRENCH—)
                           in the earth of Europe;

when they approached the hole
to pin medals

on the puppets
they had thrown there,

they slipped in BLOOD,—

. . . AND FELL IN.

Poverty and *Privilege*
alone survived,

of all the customs of the past . . .

—Should the World
regret the War? Should I

REGRET MY LIFE?

... Let our epitaph be:

In Suffering, and Nightmare,
I woke at last

to my own nature.

.   .   .

One Sunday we decided to sleigh over to Maloja.

Kyra was glad and Vaslav was very joyful that morning.

It took us about three hours to get there; Kyra and I got very hungry during the long drive.

The road was extremely narrow during the winter, because it needed cleaning from the heavy snows, and in certain parts there was always a space to await the sleighs coming from the opposite direction.

Vaslav was as a rule a careful and excellent driver, but on this particular Sunday he did not wait, but simply *drove on into* the oncoming sleighs.

We were in danger of turning over; the horses got frightened.

The coachmen of the other sleighs cursed, but this did not make any difference.

Kyra screamed, and I begged Vaslav to be more careful, but the further we went the more fiercely he drove *against* the other sleighs.

I had to clutch on to Kyra and the sleigh to keep ourselves on.

I was furious, and said so to Vaslav.

He fixed me suddenly with a hard and metallic look which I had never seen before.

As we arrived at the Maloja Inn I ordered a meal.

We had to wait.

Vaslav asked for some bread and butter and macaroni.

"Ah, Tolstoy again," I thought, but did not say a word, and bit my lips.

Kyra was anxiously awaiting her steak, and as it was laid before her and she began to eat, Vaslav, with a quick gesture, snatched the plate away.

She began to cry from disappointment.

I exclaimed, "Now, Vaslav, please don't begin that Tolstoy nonsense again; you remember how weak you got by starving yourself on that vegetarian food. I can't stop you doing it, but I won't allow you to interfere with Kyra. The child must eat properly."

I went with Kyra to the other room to have our solitary lunch.

We drove home very quietly without a word.

.   .   .

—The second part of my ballet
Le Sacre du Printemps

is called "THE SACRIFICE."

A young girl, a virgin, is chosen
to die
so that the Spring will return,—

so that her Tribe (free
from "*pity*," "*introspection*," "*remorse*")

out of her blood
can renew itself.

The fact that the earth's renewal
requires human blood

is unquestioned; a mystery.

She is chosen, from the whirling, stamping
circle of her peers, purely by chance—;

then, driven from the circle, surrounded
by the elders, by her peers, by animal
skulls impaled on pikes,

she dances,—

         at first, in paroxysms
of Grief, and Fear:—

                again and again, she leaps (—*NOT*

as a ballerina leaps, as if she
loved the air, as if
the air were her element—)

SHE LEAPS

BECAUSE SHE HATES THE GROUND.

But then, slowly, as others
join in, she finds that there is a self

WITHIN herself

that is NOT HERSELF

impelling her to accept,—and at last
to *LEAD*,—

        THE DANCE

that is her own sacrifice . . .

—In the end, exhausted, she falls
to the ground . . .

She dies; and her last breath
is the reawakened Earth's

orgasm,—
        a little upward run on the flutes
mimicking

        (—or perhaps MOCKING—)

the god's spilling
seed . . .

The Chosen Virgin
accepts her fate: without considering it,

she knows that her Tribe,—
the Earth itself,—
        are UNREMORSEFUL

that the price of continuance
is her BLOOD:—

        she *accepts* their guilt,—

. . . *THEIR GUILT*

THAT THEY DO NOT KNOW EXISTS.

She has become, to use
our term,
        a *Saint*.

The dancer I chose for this role
detested it.

She would have preferred to do
a fandango, with a rose in her teeth . . .

The training she and I shared,—

15

training in the traditional
                    "academic" dance,—

emphasizes the illusion
                    of *Effortlessness,*
Ease, Smoothness, Equilibrium . . .

When I look into my life,
these are not the qualities
                    I find there.

Diaghilev, almost alone
in the Diaghilev Ballet, UNDERSTOOD;

though he is not now, after my marriage
and *"betrayal,"*

INTERESTED in my choreographic ambitions . . .

Nevertheless, to fill a theatre,
he can be persuaded

to *hire* me as a dancer . . .

Last night I dreamt

I was slowly climbing
a long flight of steps.

Then I saw Diaghilev
and my wife

arm in arm
climbing the steps behind me . . .

I began to hurry, so that
they would not see me.

Though I climbed
as fast as I could, the space

between us
NARROWED . . .

Soon, they were a few feet behind me,—
I could hear them laughing,

gossiping, discussing CONTRACTS
and LAWSUITS . . .

They understood each other perfectly.

I stopped.

   But they

DIDN'T STOP . . .

They climbed right past me,—
laughing, chatting,

NOT SEEING ME AT ALL . . .

—I should have been happy;

yet . . .
  wasn't.

I watched their backs,
as they happily

disappeared, climbing
up, out of my sight . . .

   • • •

Our days passed in continuous social activity.

Then one Thursday, the day when the governess and maid had their day off, I was making ready to take Kyra out for a walk when suddenly Vaslav came out of his room and looked at me very angrily.

"How dare you make such a noise? I can't work."

I looked up, surprised.

His face, his manner were strange; he had never spoken to me like this.

"I am sorry. I did not realize we were so loud."

Vaslav got hold of me then by my shoulders and shook me violently.

I clasped Kyra in my arms very close, then with one powerful movement Vaslav pushed me down the stairs.

I lost my balance, and fell with the child, who began to scream.

At the bottom, I got up, more astounded than terrified.

What was the matter with him?

He was still standing there menacingly.

I turned round, exclaiming, "You ought to be ashamed! You are behaving like a drunken *peasant*."

A very changed Vaslav we found when we came home, docile and kind as ever.

I did not speak about the incident, either to him or to anybody else.

Then one day we went on an excursion and Vaslav again wore his cross over his sweater.

On our way home, he suddenly began to drive fiercely and the sleigh turned over.

Amazingly, no one was hurt.

I got really angry, and walked home with Kyra.

Of course, he was home ahead of us.

When I entered the house, the servant who worshipped Vaslav opened the door and said, "Madame, I think Monsieur Nijinsky is ill, or perhaps very drunk, for he acts so queerly. His voice is hoarse and his eyes all hazy. I am frightened."

I went to our bedroom.

Vaslav lay fully dressed on the bed, with the cross on, his eyes closed.

He seemed to be asleep.

I turned cautiously towards the door, and then noticed that heavy tears were streaming down his face.

"Vatza, how are you feeling? Are you angry with me?"

"It is nothing; let me sleep; I am tired."

.   .   .

Each night now I pray,
                    Let this cup

pass from me! . . .

But it is not a cup. It is my life.

I have *LEARNED*

                    my *NATURE* . . .

I am insane,—
. . . or evil.

Today I walked out into the snow.

I said to myself:

            THREE TIMES
YOU TRIED TO HARM YOUR WIFE AND CHILD.

I said:

        LIE DOWN IN THE SNOW
AND DIE. YOU ARE EVIL.

I lay down in the snow . . .

I tried to go to sleep.
My HANDS

began to get cold, to FREEZE.

I was lying there a long, long time.
I did not feel cold any more . . .

Then, God said to me:

GO HOME
AND TELL YOUR WIFE YOU ARE INSANE.

I said:

Thank you, thank you, God!
I am not evil. I am insane.

I got up. I wanted to go home,—
and tell this news

to my wife.

Then, I said to God:

I am insane, —
my wife will suffer. I am guilty.

Forgive me for being insane.

God said:

GOD MADE YOU. GOD DOES NOT CARE
IF YOU ARE "GUILTY" OR NOT.

I said:

I CARE IF I AM GUILTY!

I CARE IF I AM GUILTY! . . .

God was silent.

Everything was SILENT.

I lay back down in the snow.

I wanted again to go to sleep, and die . . .

But my BODY did not want to die.
My BODY spoke to me:

There is no answer to your life.
You are insane; or evil.

There is only one thing that you can do:—

You must join YOUR GUILT

to the WORLD'S GUILT.

I said to myself:

I must join MY GUILT

to the WORLD'S GUILT.

I got up out of the snow.
. . . What did the words mean?

Then I realized what the words meant.

I said to myself:

You must join YOUR GUILT

to the WORLD'S GUILT.

There is no answer to your life.
You are insane; or evil.

. . . Let this be the Body

through which the War has passed.

       .   .   .

Nijinsky invited guests to a recital at the Suvretta House Hotel.

    When the audience was seated, he picked up a chair, sat down on it, and stared at them. Half an hour passed. Then he took a few rolls of black and white velvet and made a big cross the length of the room. He stood at the head of it, his arms opened wide. He said: "Now, I will dance you the War, which you did not prevent and for which you are responsible." His dance reflected battle, horror, catastrophe, apocalypse. An observer wrote: "At the end, we were too much overwhelmed to applaud. We were looking at a corpse, and our silence was the silence that enfolds the dead."

    There was a collection for the Red Cross. Tea was served. Nijinsky never again performed in public.

       .   .   .

—The War is a *good* subject . . .

The audience, yesterday, liked
my dance.

The public does not understand *Art*;
it wants to be astonished.

I know how to astonish.

The War allowed me
to project,—
         to EMBODY,—

an ultimate *"aspect"* of the *"self"* . . .

A member of the audience told me
I had always been able

"to smell a good subject."

God, on the other hand,—

        who at times
has responded to my predilection

for *ACTIONS*

that are *METAPHYSICAL EXPERIMENTS,*—

perhaps felt threatened, or even
coerced—;

he perhaps felt that though he could
agree with me

that expiation *IS* necessary,—

he had to agree with
Nietzsche

that expiation is *NOT* possible . . .

In any case, he has chosen,—as
so often,—
    CAMOUFLAGE . . .

Now that the War has been over
two months, at times I almost
doubt if it existed—;

in truth,
          it never existed,—

. . . BECAUSE IT HAS NEVER BEEN OVER.

Twenty years ago, a boy of nine
was taken by his mother

to the Imperial School of Ballet,

to attempt to become a pupil;

the mother was poor, and
afraid of life; his father

had abandoned the family when the boy was four . . .

Even then, he had a good jump—;
he was admitted.

He had been taught by the priests
that because of Adam and Eve, all men were born
in *Original Sin,—*

          that all men were,
BY NATURE, guilty . . .

In his soul, he didn't believe it.

He was a good boy. His mother loved him.

He believed
in his essential innocence,—

he thought his nature
          GOOD . . .

He worked hard. He grew thinner,—
and started

       "dancing like God" . . .

Everyone talked about it.

But then,—
       he LEARNED SOMETHING.

He learned that

       All life exists

at the expense of other life . . .

When he began to succeed,
he saw that he was AMBITIOUS,—
              JEALOUS
of the roles that others won . . .

—Then his brother
got sick . . .

THE ROCK
       THAT GIVES SHADE TO ONE CREATURE,—

FOR ANOTHER CREATURE

       JUST BLOCKS THE SUN.

. . . This is a problem of *BEING.*
           I can imagine

no *SOLUTION* to this . . .

At sixteen, he met a Prince. He loved the Prince,—
but after a time

the Prince grew tired of him . . .

Then he met a Count—;
                      whom he *didn't* love.

The Count gave him a piano . . .

He had heard of Diaghilev. Diaghilev
invited him
            to the *Hotel Europe,*—

he went to seek his luck.

He found
his luck.

At once, he allowed Diaghilev
to make love to him.

Even then, he disliked Diaghilev
for his too self-assured voice . . .

He always had thought he was essentially
different from the people
                      in books of HISTORY,—

with their lives of *betrayals; blindness;
greed;* and *miseries* . . .

He saw, one day, that this illusion,—
this FAITH,—

              had, imperceptibly,

vanished—;

              he was NOT different—;

he did not understand *WHY* he did
what he did, nor were his instincts

"GOOD" . . .

Then, I said to myself:

"HISTORY *IS* HUMAN NATURE—;

TO SAY *I AM GUILTY*
                    IS TO ACCEPT IMPLICATION

IN THE HUMAN RACE . . ."

—Now, for months and months,
I have found

ANOTHER MAN in me—;

HE is *NOT* me—; *I*

am afraid of him . . .

He hates my wife and child,—
and hates Diaghilev;

because he thinks GOODNESS and BEING
are incompatible,—

. . . *HE WANTS TO DESTROY THE WORLD.*

DESTROY it,—
          or REDEEM it.

Are they the *same?* . . .

As a child, I was taught, by the priests,
to crave the Last Judgment:—

when the *Earth* will become a *Stage*,—

and WHAT IS RIGHT and WHAT IS WRONG

will at last show *clear*, and *distinct*,
and *separate*,—

and then,—

        THE SLATE IS WIPED CLEAN . . .

—Even now, I can see the World
wheeling on its axis . . . I

shout at it:—

        CEASE. CHANGE,—

                OR CEASE.

The World says right back:—

*I must chop down the Tree of Life
to make coffins . . .*

Tomorrow, I will go to Zurich—
to live in an asylum.

MY SOUL IS SICK,—

        NOT MY MIND.

I *am* incurable . . . I did not
live long.

Death came
unexpectedly,—

        for I wanted it to come.

Romola. Diaghilev.

. . . I HAVE EATEN THE WORLD.

My life is the expiation for my life.

Nietzsche understood me.

When *he* was sick,—when his SOUL
was sick,—
                he wrote that he would have

much preferred to be a *Professor* at Basel

than *God*—;
                but that he did not dare to carry

his egotism
so far as to neglect the Creation of the World.

        .   .   .

In 1923, Diaghilev came to see him. Vaslav by now got out of bed
in a strange fashion. First of all he went on all-fours; then crawled
around the room; and only then stood upright. In a general way,
he seemed attracted by the floor, to feel a need to be as low down
as possible (his bed was almost on a level with the floor) and to
grab hold of something. As he walked he leaned forward and felt
at his ease only when lying down.

    This was the first time Diaghilev had set eyes on him since they
had parted in wrath in Barcelona six years before. "Vatza, you are
being lazy. Come, I need you. You must dance again for the
Russian Ballet and for me."

    Vaslav shook his head. "I cannot because I am mad."

        .   .   .

Frightened to eat with a new set of teeth;
exhausted by the courage the insane have shown;
uncertain whether to REDEEM or to DESTROY THE EARTH,

—the Nineteenth Century's
guilt, *World War One,*

was danced

by Nijinsky on January 19, 1919.

FOR MARY
ANN YOUNGREN

Mary Ann, as they handed you the cup
near the black waters of Lethe,

(the cup of *Forgetfulness,*
the waters of *Obliteration,*)

did you reach for it greedily—

just as, alive, you abruptly needed

not to answer the phone for days: ballet tickets
unused: awake all night: pacing

the apartment: untouchable: chain-smoking?

Dip a finger into the River of Time,—
it comes back
        STAINED.

      .

No, that's *not* enough,—
not true, wrong—

dying of cancer, eager to have the whole thing
over, you nonetheless waited

for your sister to arrive from California
before you died,—

you needed to bring up your cruelest, worst
adolescent brutality, asking:

DO YOU FORGIVE ME?

Then: WILL YOU MISS ME?

At the Resurrection of the Dead,
the world will hear us say

The phone is plugged in, please call,
I will answer it.

CATULLUS: ODI ET AMO

I hate *and* love. Ignorant fish, who even
wants the fly while writhing.

CONFESSIONAL

Is she dead?

Yes, she is dead.

Did you forgive her?

No, I didn't forgive her.

Did she forgive you?

No, she didn't forgive me.

What did you have to forgive?

She was never mean, or willfully
cruel, or unloving.

When I was eleven, she converted to Christ—

she began to simplify her life, denied
herself, and said that she and I must struggle

"to divest ourselves
of the love of CREATED BEINGS,"—

and to help me to do that,

one day

        she hanged my cat.

I came home from school, and in the doorway
of my room,

my cat was hanging strangled.

She was in the bathroom; I could hear
the water running.

—I shouted at her;

                she wouldn't
come out.

       She was in there
for hours, with the water running . . .

Finally, late that night,
she unlocked the door.

              She wouldn't look at me.

She said that we must learn to rest
in the LORD,—

and not in His CREATION . . .

       Did you forgive her?

Soon, she had a breakdown;
when she got out of the hospital,

she was SORRY . . .

For years she dreamed the cat
had dug
its claws into her thumbs:—

in the dream, she knew, somehow,
that it was dying; she tried

to help it,—

       TO PUT IT OUT OF ITS MISERY,—

so she had her hands around its
neck, strangling it . . .

       Bewildered,

it looked at her,

       KNOWING SHE LOVED IT—;

and she *DID* love it, which was
what was
       so awful . . .

All it could do was
hold on,—
       . . . AS
SHE HELD ON.

       Did you forgive her?

I was the center of her life,—
and therefore,
of her fears and obsessions. They changed;

one was money.

. . . DO I HAVE TO GO INTO IT?

Did you forgive her?

Standing next to her coffin, looking down
at her body, I suddenly
knew I hadn't—;

               over and over
I said to her,

          I didn't forgive you!
          I didn't forgive you!

I *did* love her . . . Otherwise,

would I feel so guilty?

What did she have to forgive?

She was SORRY. She *tried*
to change . . .

She loved me. She was generous.

I pretended
that I had forgiven her—;

               and she pretended
to believe it,—

she needed desperately to believe it . . .

37

SHE KNEW I COULD BARELY STAND TO BE AROUND HER.

Did you forgive her?

I *tried*—;
      for years I almost
convinced myself I did . . .

But no, I didn't.

—Now, after I have said it all, so I can
rest,

     will you give me ABSOLUTION,—

. . . and grant this
             "created being"

FORGIVENESS? . . .

Did she forgive you?

I think she tried—;
           but no,—
she *couldn't* forgive me . . .

WHY COULDN'T SHE FORGIVE ME?

Don't you understand even now?

No! Not—not really . . .

Forgiveness doesn't exist.

II

She asked,—

       and I could not, WOULD NOT give . . .

—That is the first of two sentences
I can't get out of my head.

They somehow contain what happened.

The second is:—

THERE WAS NO PLACE IN NATURE WE COULD MEET.

     Can you explain them?

Augustine too

       had trouble with his mother,—

. . . LISTEN.

      Confessor
incapable of granting *"rest"* or *"absolution,"*—

LISTEN . . .

     Why are you angry?

Augustine too

       had trouble with his mother,—

but the story of Augustine and Monica
is the *opposite* of what happened

between me and my mother . . .

We couldn't meet in Nature,—

. . . AND ALL WE HAD WAS NATURE.

       How do you explain it?

The scene at the window at Ostia
in Book Nine of the *Confessions*

seems designed to make non-believers

sick with envy . . .

—You are listening to a soul
                    that has *always* been

SICK WITH ENVY . . .

       How do you explain it?

As a child I was (now, I
clearly can see it)

            PREDATORY,—

pleased to have supplanted my father
in my mother's affections,

and then pleased to have supplanted my stepfather . . .

—I assure you, though I was a *"little boy,"*
I could be far more charming, sympathetic,
full of sensibility, *"various,"* far more
an understanding and feeling
ear for my mother's emotions, needs, SOUL

than any man, any man she met,—

I know I *wanted* to be: WANTED
to be the center, the focus of her life . . .

I was her ally against my father;
and then, after the first two or three

years, her ally against my stepfather . . .

—Not long before she died,
she told me something
                        I had never heard,—

when I was nine or ten, early
in her second marriage,

she became pregnant; she said she
wanted to have the child . . .

She said that one day, when my stepfather
was playing golf, she was out walking the course

with him, and suddenly

a man fell from one of the huge trees
lining the fairways . . .

A group of men had been cutting limbs;
she saw one of them fall,

                              and for a long time

lie there screaming.

Later that day, she had a miscarriage . . .

—After saying all this, she
looked at me insistently and said,

"I wanted to have the child."

But as she was telling me the story,
I kept thinking

THANK GOD THE MAN FELL,
THANK GOD SHE SAW HIM FALL AND HAD A MISCARRIAGE

AND THE CHILD DIED . . .

—I felt sick. I knew I was *GLAD*
the man fell, *GLAD* she saw him fall

and the child died . . .

—When I was nine or ten, if she
had had a child—; if

she and a child and my stepfather
had made a FAMILY

from which I *had* to be closed off,
the remnant of a rejected, erased past,—

(I never had anything in common with,
or even RESPECTED, my stepfather,—)

I would have gone crazy . . .

—How could she have *BETRAYED ME*
in that way? . . .

How do you explain it?

I felt sick. I felt ill at how
PREDATORY I was,—

(my feelings *STILL* were,—)

at the envy and violence I could
will NOT to feel,

but *COULDN'T* not feel . . .

—Augustine has the temerity, after
his mother dies,

to admit he is GLAD
she no longer wanted to be buried

next to her husband . . .

He thanks God
for ridding her of this "vain desire."

Why are you angry?

In the words of Ecclesiastes:—

"Her loves, her hates, her jealousies,—

                                             these all

have perished, nor will she EVER AGAIN

TAKE PART
in whatever is done under the sun . . ."

My mother,—

      . . . *JUST DIED.*

The emotions, the *"issues"* in her life
didn't come out somewhere, reached no culmination,
climax, catharsis,—

      she *JUST DIED.*

She wanted them to—;
           how can I talk about

the way in which, when I was young,

we seemed to be engaged in an ENTERPRISE
together,—

      the enterprise of "figuring out the world,"
figuring out her life, my life,—

THE MAKING OF HER SOUL,

         which somehow, in our "enterprise"
together, was the making of my soul,—

. . . it's a kind of CRAZINESS, which some mothers
drink along with their children
        in their *MOTHER'S-MILK* . . .

Why are you angry?

THERE WAS NO PLACE IN NATURE WE COULD MEET . . .

—I've never let anyone else
in so deeply . . .

But when the predatory complicit co-conspirator
CHILD

was about twenty, he of course wanted his *"freedom,"*—

and then he found

that what had made his life
possible, what he found so deeply INSIDE HIM,

had its hands around his neck,
                              strangling him,—

and that therefore, if he were
to survive,

he must in turn strangle, murder,
kill it inside him . . .

TO SURVIVE, I HAD TO KILL HER INSIDE ME.

Why are you angry?

Now that she is dead (that her BODY
is DEAD),

I'm capable of an *"empathy,"*

an *"acceptance"* of the INEVITABLE
(in her, and in myself)

that I denied her, living . . .

I DENIED HER, LIVING.

She asked,—

and I could not, WOULD NOT give . . .

I *did* "will" to forgive her, but

FORGIVENESS lay beyond the will,—

. . . and I willed NOT to forgive her,
for "forgiveness" seems to say:—

Everything is forgotten, obliterated,—
the past

is as nothing, erased . . .

Her plea, her need for forgiveness
seemed the attempt to obliterate

the ACTIONS, ANGERS, DECISIONS

that *made me* what I am . . .

To obliterate the CRISES, FURIES, REFUSALS
that are how I
came to UNDERSTAND her—; me—;

my life . . .

Truly to feel "forgiveness,"
to forgive her *IN MY HEART,*

meant erasing *ME* . . .

—She seemed to ask it to render me paralyzed,
and defenseless . . .

Now that I no longer must face her,
I give her in my mind

the "*empathy*" and "*acceptance*"

I denied her, living.

Why are you angry?

. . . But if, somehow, WHAT WE WERE
didn't have to be understood

by MEMORY,

and THIS EARTH,—

. . . Augustine and Monica,

as they lean
alone together standing at a window

overlooking a garden at the center of the house
(in Book Nine of the *Confessions*),

near the time of her death (which time,
Augustine says, GOD knew,

though they did not),—

resting here at Ostia from a long journey
by land,

47

and preparing for a long sea-journey
back to the Africa which is their home,—

. . . as they stand here sweetly talking together,
and ask

      "what the eternal life of the saints could be"

(panting to be sprinkled from the waters of God's fountain
to help them meditate
                upon so great a matter),—

. . . as they stand alone together
at this window,

      they can FORGET THE PAST

AND LOOK FORWARD

           TO WHAT LIES BEFORE THEM . . .

—They had much to forget;

in the *Confessions,* Monica's ferocity
is frightening:—

      before Augustine became a Christian,
she saw him as dead—;

she refused to live with him or even
eat at the same table in his house,
shunning and detesting his blasphemies,—

until she had a dream in which she
learned that he would finally convert to Christ . . .

—When he planned to leave Africa for Italy,
she was determined he would take her
with him, or remain at home;

she followed him to the seacoast,
clinging to him, he says, with *"dreadful grief"*;

one night he escaped,
                    and sailed,—

not long after, she followed . . .

—Finally, of course, he became a Christian;
until then, she
ceaselessly wept and mourned and prayed . . .

            Do you know why you are saying all this?

As Augustine and Monica stood leaning at that
window in Ostia, contemplating

what the saints' possession of God is like,

they moved past and reviewed
(Augustine tells us)

                    each level of created things,—

each level of CREATION, from this earth
to the sun and moon and stars

shining down on this earth . . .

—Talking, musing, wondering
at Creation, but knowing that our life and light

here cannot compare

to the sweetness of the saints' LIGHT and LIFE,—

(here, where he had forced her to *SEEK*
what out of her body she had herself

brought forth,—)

. . . now, self-gathered at last in the purity of their own
being, they ascend higher

still, and together SCALE THE STARS . . .

—And so, Augustine tells us, they came to their own Souls,—

and then went
past them, to that region of richness

unending, where God feeds ISRAEL forever
with the food of Truth . . .

There LIFE is the WISDOM
by which all things are made, which

itself is *not* made . . .

—While they were thus talking of, straining to comprehend,
panting for this WISDOM, with all the effort

of their heart, for one heartbeat,

they together attained to *touch* it—;

. . . then sighing, and leaving the first-fruits
of their Spirit bound there,

they returned to the sound of their own voice,—
to WORDS,

which have a beginning and an end . . .

"How unlike," Augustine says, "God's WORD,—
changeless, self-gathered, unmade, yet forever

making all things new . . ."

How do you explain it?

Then they said:—
                    "If any man could shut his ears

to the tumult of the flesh—;

                              if suddenly the cacophony
of earth and sea and air

were SILENT, and the voice of the self
died to the self, and so the self

found its way beyond the self,—

beyond the SELF it has made,—

                    SILENT
our expiations and confessions,
the voice that says: *NO REMISSION OF SINS
WITHOUT THE SHEDDING OF BLOOD,*

the WORD that was only given us drenched in blood,—

. . . if to any man

his Self, CREATION ITSELF

(Substance and Accidents and their Relations)

suddenly were SILENT,—

                              and in that silence,

he then heard CREATION
                              say with one voice:—

We are not our own source,—
                              even those of us

who made ourselves, creatures
of the Will, the Mirror, and the Dream,

know we are not our own source,—

. . . if he heard this voice,
                              and then

all Creation were, even for a second, SILENT,—

(this Creation in which creatures
of consciousness,

                  whose LAW is that they come to be
through CHANGE, through
birth, fruition, and death,

know that as they move toward fullness
of being, they move toward ceasing to be,—)

. . . if in this SILENCE,

He whom we *crave* to hear

SPOKE AT LAST—;

spoke not through the VEIL
of earth and sea and air,

thunder, 'SIGNS AND WONDERS,' the voice
of an angel, the enigma of similitude and of

parable, all

the ALIEN that BESETS us here,—

. . . spoke not by them, but by HIMSELF,

calling us to return into that secret place from
which He

        comes forth at last to us,—

. . . just as we two
together reached forth and for one

heartbeat attained to *TOUCH*

the *WISDOM* that is our *SOURCE* and *GROUND*,—

. . . if this could continue, and LIFE
were that one moment of
               wisdom and understanding

for which we then sighed,—

would not *this* be: *ENTER THOU INTO THE JOY OF THY LORD?* . . .

And when shall it be? At
the Resurrection of the Dead, when all
shall rise, but not all shall be changed?

And shall *we* then be changed? . . ."

In words like these, but not
exactly these, (Augustine then says,)

they talked together that day—

(just as the words I have given you are
not, of course, exactly Augustine's).

Monica then said,
                    "Son, I no longer hope

for anything from this world.

I wanted to stay alive long enough
to see you a Catholic Christian.

God has granted me this, in
superabundance.

. . . What am I still doing here?"

In five days, she fell into a fever;
nine days later she was dead.

                Why are you angry?

My mother, at the end of her life, was *frightened*.

She was afraid to die
not because she feared an afterlife,

but because she didn't know what her life had been.

Her two marriages were failures,—

she stayed married to my stepfather, but
in despair, without trust in or respect for him, or

visible affection . . .

She had had no profession,—

she had painted a few paintings, and
written a handful of poems, but without the illusion

either were any good, or STOOD FOR HER . . .

She had *MADE* nothing.

I was what she had made.—

She saw that her concern and worry and care
in the end called up in me

protestations of affection
that veiled

       unappeasable anger, and remorse.

UNDOING THIS was beyond me . . .

She felt she was here for some REASON,—
. . . but never found it.

     Man needs a metaphysics;
     he cannot have one.

THE SACRIFICE

When Judas writes the history of SOLITUDE,—
. . . let him celebrate

Miss Mary Kenwood; who, without
help, placed her head in a plastic bag,

then locked herself
in a refrigerator.

.

—Six months earlier, after thirty years
teaching piano, she had watched

her mother slowly die of throat cancer.
Watched her *want* to die . . .

What once had given Mary life
in the end didn't want it.

Awake, her mother screamed for help to die.
—She felt

GUILTY . . . She knew that *all* men in these situations felt
innocent—; helpless—; yet guilty.

.

Christ knew the Secret. Betrayal
is necessary; as is woe for the betrayer.

The solution, Mary realized at last,
must be brought out of my own body.

Wiping away our sins, Christ stained us with his blood—;
to offer yourself, yet need *betrayal,* by *Judas,* before SHOULDERING

THE GUILT OF THE WORLD—;
. . . *Give me the courage not to need Judas.*

     .

When Judas writes the history of solitude,
let him record

that to the friend who opened
the refrigerator, it seemed

death fought; before giving in.

GENESIS 1–2:4

In the beginning, God made HEAVEN and EARTH.

The earth without form was waste.

DARKNESS was the face of the deep.
His spirit was the wind brooding over the waters.

.

In darkness he said,
                    LET THERE BE LIGHT.

There was light.

In light he said, IT IS GOOD.

God, dividing darkness from light,
named light DAY and darkness NIGHT.

Night and day were the first day.

.

God said,
          LET THE FIRMAMENT

ARC THE EARTH.

The waters opened.

        The ARC above the earth
divided the waters above from the waters below.

God named the arc, HEAVEN.

Night and day were the second day.

    .

God said,
        LET THE WATERS BELOW THE FIRMAMENT

RECEDE, REVEALING THE GROUND.

The waters opened, and receded.
What lay beneath the waters was the GROUND.

God named the dry ground, EARTH.
He named the waters surrounding the earth, OCEAN.

God looked.
        He said, IT IS GOOD.

God said,
        LET THE BARE EARTH

BREAK OPEN, HEAVY WITH SEED.

The earth broke open.
                Numberless PLANTS filled

with seed spread over the ground, and TREES
boughed with fruit heavy with seed.

God looked.
        He said, IT IS GOOD.

Night and day were the third day.

.

God said,
>LET GREAT LIGHTS IN THE FIRMAMENT

ORDER AND ILLUMINATE THE EARTH.

God placed great lights shining in the firmament,

the GREATER LIGHT to dominate the day,
the LESSER LIGHT to dominate the night,

and STARS.

God looked. He said,
>LET THEM BE FOR SIGNS.

Dividing darkness from light, the shining
made SEASONS, DAYS, YEARS.

God said, IT IS GOOD.

Night and day were the fourth day.

.

God said,
>LET THE MOVING WATERS LIVE

WITH TEEMING, LIVING CREATURES.

God said,
>LET THE EMPTY FIRMAMENT LIVE

WITH TEEMING, LIVING CREATURES.

God made the creatures of the deep,
BEASTS and MONSTERS, all those

swarming within it. God made the winged creatures
moving across the face of the firmament.

God looked.
        He said, IT IS GOOD.

God blessed them, saying,
                INCREASE. MULTIPLY.
FILL THE WATERS.
              ARCING THE EARTH,

FILL THE FIRMAMENT.

They increased and multiplied.

Night and day were the fifth day.

     .

God said,
       LET THE EARTH BRING FORTH

LIVING CREATURES BOUND TO THE EARTH.

God made the beasts of the earth,
cattle, each according to its kind.

He made the creatures that crawl on the earth,
reptiles, each according to its kind.

God looked.
        He said, IT IS GOOD.

God said,
>	LET US MAKE MAN

LIKE US, IN OUR IMAGE AND LIKENESS.

God said,
>	LET THEM DOMINATE THE EARTH,

AND THE CREATURES OF THE EARTH.

God made MAN in his own image,
in the image of God

he made him,
>	MAN and WOMAN
he made them.

Of one likeness
>	MALE FE MALE
two he made.

God blessed them, saying,
>		INCREASE. MULTIPLY.

DOMINATE THE EARTH,

AND THE CREATURES OF THE EARTH.

God looked. He said,
>		YOUR MEAT SHALL BE

PLANTS, SEEDS, FRUIT.

God said to the man and woman
and all the creatures on the earth,

YOUR MEAT SHALL BE THE EARTH,

NOT THE CREATURES OF THE EARTH.

God looked.
            He said, IT IS VERY GOOD.

Night and day were the sixth day.

            .

God rested. On the seventh day

God rested. He looked at HEAVEN and EARTH,
and ceased.

Heaven and earth with all their panoply
were made.

God blessed the seventh day, God made
the seventh day a holy day,

because on the seventh day God rested, God ceased.

            .

This was the creation of the world.